The Kweendom™ Presents:

BOSS UP OR BITCH UP

Life Lessons a Former Teen Mom Used to Start a Business And Kill The Entrepreneurial Game

Kween Mingo

Copyright

Any use of information in this book is at the reader's discretion and risk. Neither the author or publisher can be held responsible for any loss, claim(s) and/or damages arising out of the use and/or misuse of the suggestions made, the failure to take medical advice from a trained medical professional or for any materials on third-party websites.

Dedication

For My Brother and Guardian Angel, Quantrell Keller.

Table of Contents

Girl, Don't Be Scurred (Scared)

Introduction

I must say, I am beyond excited that out of all the billions of books in the world, you have chosen this one. I'm GENUINELY ECSTATIC that you have chosen to read this book and I am so very appreciative that I can barely put my thoughts into words.

You see, I have always been the underdog. I've always felt like I was the misfit. I've always felt out of place. I wasn't considered the pretty girl in school. I wasn't considered the most popular girl. In fact, I was the nerdy girl who was cool with everyone but no one was beating down my door to have me in their clique.

Before moving to The Tampa Bay area when I was about 12 years old, I was raised in a small town in South Carolina, called Orangeburg. Back in the 90s it was pretty laid back, at least from what I remember. On the weekends I would visit my grandparents in a teeny tiny town called Elloree and that was where all the real fun took place.

Elloree was super duper small. You're practically related to everyone and there was some sort of party every weekend. Some of my best childhood memories came from my weekend visits to Elloree. I did everything from trying to drive my grandmother's car without permission (and while underaged) to trying to set a tree on fire in the backyard with my cousin. My siblings, cousins and I would ride our bikes all over the town just because we could. One time my older brother and I hopped on our bikes and just started riding. The next thing we knew, we were about 10 miles away from home in 100-degree weather and begging our mom to come get us. And of course, she refused but it was these very moments that were the BEST TIMES OF MY LIFE and helped mold me into the woman I am today.

Throughout the years I've made some decisions that weren't ideal. But the events that took after I made those decisions are also the reasons why I am so determined and ambitious. When I have it in my mind to do something, I go at it relentlessly and it has turned out to be financially lucrative for me.

One of my biggest decisions was when I chose to leave my 9-5 as a paralegal within a law firm and start my own paralegal firm. Doing so afforded me a lifestyle that I would only see in the movies. The freedom I earned has been a huge blessing to me. But after helping attorneys amass an estimated $50 million in attorney's fees, I decided to branch off and help my soul sistas do the same. This is how *Freedom of The Kweendom*™ was born!

The purpose of this book is to show "everyday" women like me that you can use your experiences in your life to discover your passions and live the life you want. Only you can determine what that life looks like. Maybe you want to be an entrepreneur. Maybe you want to be a stay at home mom. Perhaps you're more interested in returning to school to become a neurosurgeon. Whatever it is you want to do, DO IT!

As you go through the book, I want you to read and meditate on the affirmations. Don't just look at the words. Read it. Soak it in. Believe it. Highlight it. Write it down. Do what you need to do to begin to live by these affirmations. Also, complete the action plans at the end of each chapter.

Now, before we take a deep dive into discovering your passion and turning it into a paycheck, I want you to clear your mind of clutter. Clear your mind of all the negative things you have been feeding it. I want you to become optimistic and understand if I can go from being a teen mom, wiping booties for a living (NO SHADE TO ANYONE. I was a caregiver in a nursing home at one time) to having several businesses and owning an abundance of real estate, you can too. Whatever you want to do in life, you can! Don't for a second doubt your abilities. Believe in yourself and make no excuses.

Now, let's get started.

Affirmation #1

I am in charge, and I take complete ownership of power!

Chapter 1

What's Holding You Back?

What is the one thing you want in life that seems to be farfetched? What is the one dream you have that you're afraid to tell anyone out of fear of judgment?

Now, imagine what it would be like if this dream of yours could come true! How would you feel? Would it change your quality of life? Would you be able to live a life of freedom? Would this dream enable you to live life in the manner that you choose? Would this dream allow you to fly private jets? Perhaps, you would own a jet. How would this dream change your life?

Now, think about why you haven't started to pursue this dream? What excuses are you telling yourself? Who are you afraid of disappointing? What are you afraid of? Why are you making excuses? Are you afraid of failure? Are you afraid of what people will say if you fail? Be honest with yourself because honesty is what is going to make this dream become a reality.

Action Step:

Get a journal that will be specifically dedicated to completing the action steps in this book. It doesn't have to be fancy. It can be a regular notebook from your local Dollar Tree, or you can give it a touch of your personality with a journal from my online store, Kween's Kloset (KweensKloset.com).

Affirmation #2

I have the power to change the world, and I will do so by following my passion.

Chapter 2

Discover your passion

As a child, I always knew I wanted to be a married, mom who happened to be an attorney that "helped people get out of jail." Here, I am, roughly 30 years later and I am a married, mom who happens to be an owner of several businesses, one of which is a paralegal company.

Over the years, my passions have changed. While I still have an insanely passionate love for helping people, I do it in other various ways. My paralegal company helps in many different forms; the injured are able to recover financially, attorneys earn a living, other paralegals learn various aspects of the personal injury process and so much more. Also, I have a 501(c)3 non-profit organization, Konfidence of a Kween, which helps the community in many different forms. We do everything from providing business grants to hosting missionary trips. I teach people how to start their own business and be able to live a life of freedom (i.e.: Freedom of The

Kweendom™), and so much more. One thing that is pleasantly consistent is I can help other people with every single one of my business and THAT brings me joy.

Now, think back to when you were a child. What interested you? Are you still living in that purpose? Are you enjoying waking up every morning and heading into your office? Are you only working for the money? Do you dread Sunday nights? Do you hate the sound of your alarm clock? If some of these resonate with you, odds are you aren't living in your purpose. You aren't doing something that brings you excitement. Do you even know what excites you? Well, grab your notebook and let's figure this out, sis.

Action Plan:

1. What did you enjoy doing as a child? Sure, things change as you get older but if you dig deep and think, you may discover your passion.
2. If life didn't require money or bartering to survive, how would you spend your time? Before writing down your answer, I want you to think about this. And to

take things a tad bit further, let's also say you can't just sit at home and do nothing. You must go out into the world and do something of value. What would you do?

3. Are there any social issues that you sincerely care about in your heart? What gets you worked up? What makes you want to argue your point all day and night.

4. What activity can you do that makes you forget about the time? What gets you completely lost?

5. What is something you couldn't possibly imagine not doing in life? Maybe it's cooking. Perhaps it's being with your children every day. Or perhaps it is talking to your friends. Just be honest and write down what you couldn't possibly imagine doing in life.

6. What do you hate doing? What tasks do you always find yourself putting off? What job duties do you loathe? Answering these questions may help narrow down your true passions.

7. Use your imagination; visualize your alarm clock going off and you hurrying out of bed with boatloads of excitement.

What would cause such excitement? What would make you want to jump out of your bed and head into "work"?

8. Describe your biggest nightmare in life? (It's good to know what you don't want as well).

9. Who are your most prominent models and why?

10. What makes you happy? Sis, list it ALL!

11. What is it that you could do to change the world, that would make you cry tears of joy?

12. What have you personally gone through that you would like to keep other people from enduring?

13. If no one else could say anything negative about your actions, what would you be doing?

14. WHAT is the most essential THING in your life? Not your boo. Not your kids. Not any person but THING.

15. If you woke up tomorrow and were 200 years old, what would you regret not doing?

16. Over the last week, what gave you the most joy, love and/or satisfaction?

17. What is one thing you would tell your best friend to do before leaving this world?
18. Who are you most grateful for and why? List everyone, boo!
19. Up until this point in your life, what is your biggest regret?
20. What special gift do you have that you could give to the entire world?

Life Lesson For Business:

It's ok to change your mind about your path but continue to follow your passions.

Affirmation #3

I won't ever give up. Not today. Not tomorrow. Not ever!

Chapter 3

Don't Quit. No Matter What.

What if I said to you everything you want in life is within your reach? Would you believe me? What if I told you no matter how big or how small your dreams are, you can achieve your aspirations? What if I told you, failure does not exist? Would you pursue your dreams?

Well, boo, everything I said is 100% true. Your dreams are within reach. You can achieve even the most outlandish dreams you can fathom. Failure does not exist. But to succeed, you must be able to push yourself further than you are currently imagining. When faced with resistance, chaos, lack of money, fear, lack of time and any other opposition, you must persevere and keep going.

If your spouse doesn't believe in your dream, you must continue to go. If you aren't feeling well, even though you have to take care of yourself and know your limit, you still have to keep going. If you are overwhelmed and currently underpaid, you must keep going because everything you want in life is within reach.

I met my husband, Tim in 2006. At the time, I was a single mom who had just been laid off. I was a young 20-year-old girl, who was living in a small two bedroom condo with my daughter, Kianna. I had dreams of becoming a high powered attorney, and I was a few weeks away from getting my Associates Degree in Paralegal Studies.

I met Tim in the middle of the dance floor at one of the most ratchet nightclubs in Ybor City, a small historic neighborhood in Tampa, Fl. He walked up to me and after we exchanged a few words, I reluctantly provided him with a phone number. I had just broken up with my boyfriend and wasn't looking for another stupid boy to occupy my time. So it's no shock that I initially gave him the wrong phone number. But, as luck would have it, my information didn't save in his phone, so he asked me to try again. I hesitated for a second and then asked him, "why should I give him my number?" And as corny as this sounds, his response changed my entire life. He responded by saying, "because I'm special."

No one had ever said that to me before. Usually, the boys would say something stupid or vulgar which would immediately turn me off, and I would give him the wrong information. Tim, on the other hand, was nerdy but seemed genuine and this caught my attention. So, I gave him the correct information.

A week after giving Tim my number, he finally called me. I had forgotten all about him and didn't even remember giving him my information, so I became curious and wanted to see him.

I met up with Tim later that evening and after going for a ride with him down Ybor City's strip, it became apparent that Tim and I weren't cut out to be a couple. He was cool as a friend and I remember telling my mother that I could totally see us becoming best friends. And we did.

Over the course of several weeks or so, I started to feel funny. Tim and I had become really good friends. We would talk about dating life. He would tell me about a girl he was dating. I would tell him about a guy I was dating. It was nice having a man's perspective on my dating life, but I was really starting to dig this nerdy guy. I told one of my best friends Tim would be my husband one day. And then, we started dating exclusively.

After getting to know Tim, it was evident that music was his passion. He loved every second of it, and I was okay with being with someone whose dreams were utterly different than mine. Up to this point, I wanted to marry a professional such as a doctor or accountant.

Tim and I were together for just over a year when I convinced him to move to Atlanta, Georgia. He had already made a name for himself in Tampa and he was perfectly fine being considered a "Tampa Legend". But I had bigger dreams for him. I knew he had the potential to have more than just a hit song in Tampa. I knew he had the potential to make everyone in the entire world move to the beat of his drums. I believed in him when he didn't even believe in himself.

July 27, 2007, we moved to Atlanta, Georgia. It was difficult and our relationship was tested. I was having a hard time finding a job and I felt like I was a burden on Tim, but it wasn't long before life began to head in a positive direction.

November 2007, almost four full months after moving to Atlanta, I started working at one of Georgia's most prominent personal injury law firms. I loved it! I was the youngest paralegal in that particular office and I was a bit spoiled. I was given the name "Princess" and it just stuck with me - until I got married and became a *Kween*. The law firm was laid back and a lot of fun. I enjoyed my colleagues and I genuinely enjoyed the work. But on the other hand, Tim was in a slump.

He was renting a room in a building in Midtown Atlanta as his studio. It was bringing in money, but not what he was accustomed to earning. Additionally, because he now had more expenses since he was no longer living in his parents' home, he began to feel the effects of not being the "breadwinner". I loved Tim (obviously, I still do) so I didn't mind picking up the slack. We simply carried on and continued to build a life together.

July 2, 2011, Tim and I married at Cherokee Run Golf & Country Club. It was the second happiest day of my life, up to that point (the first being the day I gave birth to my daughter, Kianna). I was on top of the world on my wedding day and even now, years later, some days I wish I could do it all over again.

Naturally, following the wedding, we wanted to expand our family. We both wanted to have four more children and decided we would work on it during our honeymoon in the Florida Keys. Unfortunately, having babies wasn't exactly an easy task.

After trying to get pregnant for over a year, I saw a specialist who informed me I was suffering from Polycystic Ovary Syndrome (PCOS) and I also had severe scar tissue from my c-section with Kianna, as well as endometriosis. Things looked grim.

We continued to try to get pregnant and then finally, in January 2013, we got pregnant! Our first doctor's appointment, we were ecstatic to get our ultrasound and see our little baby. But when I woke up March 5, 2013, to bleeding, I knew what was happening. We went in to have an ultrasound only to find out we were pregnant with twins and neither baby had a heartbeat! Talk about bone crushing! I wanted to curl in a ball and cry my eyes out. So I did.

But, I'm no quitter, so we tried again. And to our surprise, we got pregnant again, almost immediately. We were cautiously excited.

In May, one of my grandmothers passed away. I was devastated. I tried my best not to get too upset because I did not want to lose my baby. But, unfortunately about a week after my grandmother passed away, Tim and I went in for our ultrasound and the baby did not have a heartbeat. I went into a full-on rage! I'm talking about yelling, screaming, kicking, cursing and everything else you can imagine. It was pretty ugly.

When I didn't miscarry naturally, I had to have a Dilation and Curettage procedure. It was painful and I was pissed. I opted to have the tissue of my baby tested to see if there was anything I could have done to prevent this miscarriage.

The day my really good friend, Freda and I were scheduled to see The Queen (Beyoncé), the nurse at the doctor's office called me with my results. She confirmed *my son* was a healthy baby boy with no genetic issues, etc. She stated she was not sure why I miscarried. This killed my spirit. Knowing I was would have had a son, made everything seem so much more real, which hurt even more. It broke me. I'm literally in tears thinking about it now.

After getting this news, I knew the doctors were missing something. I just knew it! So, I started my own research. The first thing I thought about was how I had a placenta abruption with Kianna. I remember when my doctor came to me after I gave birth to Kianna, she stated the placenta was riddled with blood clots! That was my *Aha Moment!* BLOOD CLOTS!

At that moment, I remembered I had previously had substantial medical tests done during the time we were having difficulty conceiving, and when I had a car accident a few months later, I had ordered my medical records. So I spent an entire weekend combing through my medical records, and as a personal injury paralegal, I was well trained in skimming medical records but desperate times cause for extreme measures and I could not miss anything!

BOOM

There it was! Right in my medical records, it clearly stated I was suffering from a blood clotting disorder called Methylenetetrahydrofolate Reductase (MTHFR). This genetic condition can cause blood clots during pregnancy. It doesn't affect everyone the same but it obviously was causing my miscarriages, right?

It was a Sunday evening when I found this info, so I immediately emailed my specialist. I also called my mom and my closest friends. I was ecstatic. And girl, when I found out about the treatment, I was at a loss for words. Do you know what could have prevented me from losing THREE BABIES?! Metformin (used for Diabetes), Folate, and a baby aspirin!

Fast-forward to January 2014, and we are pregnant again, with twins! I was again cautiously excited, but I felt better because we had a treatment plan. I was still working in the legal field but at a different firm and Tim's music was picking up. By this time, he had already worked with several great artists such as Doe B (R.I.P.), 2pistols, T-Pain and more. Tim was a bit concerned about having two more people to take care of and provide for financially. I didn't care. I'm a woman, so we always make a way!

September 2014, we welcomed our twins, Timia and Timothy, Jr. Kianna, Tim and I were in love! I couldn't thank God enough even if saying "Thank you" was all I said every single second for the rest of my life. The blessings I felt was just indescribable.

As time went on, Tim started to panic. I was out of work and he knew I didn't want to go back to my previous law firm. Plus, the cost of daycare wouldn't justify me going back to work full time. By November 2014, Tim was looking for a full-time job.

From the moment I met Tim, he was working for himself. He had not worked for anyone else since his college days. So because I knew he would hate working for someone else but we also needed more money, I started Paramount Paralegal Service to bring in some extra cash.

I got my first client and things seemed to be going well. Unfortunately, it wasn't enough, so Tim decided to work at a warehouse. After the first day, I told Tim to stop working there and continue his passion. It just didn't make sense for him to stop doing what he loved. Afterall, our bills were paid, we had food on the table, and we were happy. And even though we had to cut back on things, we weren't in dire need.

December of 2014, Tim produced a beat that would change our entire lives and by April of 2015, just as I had imagined, everyone across the globe was moving to the beat of his drums. The world was whipping and nae naeing as Tim produced the song "Watch Me".

Life will always have special surprises. Some we enjoy. Some we hate. How you react to these surprises determines how your life will be shaped. After I had a few miscarriages, I could have given up and given in. I didn't. I kept going. I didn't sit around, waiting for the doctors to get their shit together. Instead, I got my shit together.

When Tim wanted to get a job in a warehouse, I could have discouraged him from pursuing his dreams, goals, and aspirations. But, if I had, I don't think I would be qualified to write this book and tell you to pursue your dreams, goals, and aspirations.

Despite having to cut back on things I loved, I still encouraged Tim to keep going. And now, I am urging you to keep going. Your obstacles are just opportunities for you to get stronger. Don't quit. Keep going.

Life Lesson For Business:

Quitting is for wimps. Figure out how to make that shit work and do it. Don't sit around waiting on someone else to get the job done. Roll up your sleeves and get down to business. No excuses.

Action Plan:

Imagine what would have happened if I gave up on my dream of having more children. Imagine what would have happened if I didn't push Tim to continue to pursue his dreams. I wouldn't be writing this book. You wouldn't be reading this book. Would you be doing this action plan I am going to lay out for you? Probably not. And you certainly wouldn't be seeing those adorable little faces on my Instagram! But here we are, going through this action plan together, so let's get to it!

Get a jar, box, cup or anything that can hold small pieces of paper. Now, take out your handy, dandy notebook (Yes, I took that from Dora The Explorer - *smile*) and write out all of your dreams! I don't care if your goal is to finish this book or if it is something grander like buying a private jet, WRITE IT DOWN. Don't worry about how you're going to achieve this dream. Just write out your thoughts, goals, and ideas. When you are finished, fold the little pieces of paper and place in your jar. Every night before bed, randomly pick a piece of paper in the jar and read it to yourself. Then, visualize and pray over your dream before bed.

Affirmation #4

***I make the right choices. EVERY. SINGLE.
TIME.***

Chapter 4

Just Decide

Don't make this more difficult than it has to be. Simply decide that this is what you want. Don't waver in your decision. Vehemently decide. If your goal is to open a hair salon, simply decide to do it. Don't waver. Don't go back and forth with your decision. Just decide. If you want to buy that new Louis Vuitton bag, just decide and do it. Whatever you are questioning, just decide and do it.

Back when I was pregnant with my twins, I was working at a company that appeared to be understanding of my needs as a pregnant woman. The owner of the company never said anything morally wrong to me about being pregnant, and his female assistant didn't either. She was very understanding throughout all my ups and downs that I had experienced within a 6-month time span.

Thirteen weeks into my pregnancy, I woke up with extreme pain on my right side. It was debilitating, but for some reason, I went to work as usual. People who knew me (but didn't know I was pregnant yet) knew something was amiss and they could tell I was in agony as I was walking hunched over and much slower than usual. Several people asked me if I was ok and I started telling people that I was pregnant with twins and due to my small frame, the babies were probably hurting me (crazy, right? Stick with me, ok?).

As the day went on, the pain got progressively worse, but I kept going. That evening, I had plans to meet up with a former coworker for dinner, and because I am notorious for canceling, I decided to go anyway. Once I arrived at her place of employment, I parked my car and what would have typically been a 2-minute walk to her office, took almost 10 minutes. Once I arrived, she asked me if I was ok and once again, I told her I was pregnant with twins and wasn't feeling well. She was kind and understanding and asked if I wanted to cancel. Again, I refused.

Together, we walked to Colony Square in Midtown Atlanta. It took what seemed like an eternity, and my pain was now at about an eight on a scale of 1-10. I don't even remember much about that dinner. I just kept thinking to myself, "I can't wait for tomorrow to get here so I can go to my doctor."

After dinner, I drove home. I parked in my garage and dreaded the thought of walking up the stairs. I must have been taking too long because my husband, Tim came to the see what was wrong. He looked at me and I had tears in my eyes. I told him I was in pain and just wanted to shower and get in bed. So, I did.

Abuor 9 o'clock that night, the pain became practically unbearable. I asked Tim to take me to the hospital. He knew I was in a significant amount of pain and did what I asked.

Upon arrival at the hospital, the medical staff informed me the wait would be several hours. I was pissed. This has never happened before and I couldn't understand why it would take so long. After evaluating the situation, I decided it was best to go home and wait until the next morning to see my gynecologist.

I didn't sleep at all that night because the pain of so severe. I contemplated calling the ambulance but decided I was being dramatic.

Seven thirty the next morning, I was attempting to get my doctor on the line. When I was finally able to reach someone, they offered me an immediate appointment but it wasn't with my regular doctor that I wanted to deliver my babies. Instead, I would be seeing one of his partners. I didn't care. I just needed a doctor ASAP.

When we got to the doctor's office, an ultrasound was immediately performed. My babies were fine!

WHEW!

As a mom who had lost a few babies due to miscarriage I was nervous, so I felt I could breathe a sigh of relief knowing my babies were well. But then, the doctor informed me I had a mass on my right ovary, the size of a softball. He stated I would need surgery to remove it. Tim and I number one concern was the babies, so I told the doctor, I would take my chances with pain medication just so my babies would have a chance at survival. I will never forget his next words. The doctor looked me straight in my eyes and said, "Mrs. Mingo, I understand you have been through hell on your journey to having more children, and I understand your dilemma, but if you don't have this surgery, you will die. And because your babies aren't viable at 13 weeks, they won't survive either."

The doctor left Tim and me alone to discuss it. My husband immediately began to break down. His eyes turned bloodshot red as he fought back the tears. I became angry and told him to get it together because I needed him to be strong for both of us. I know it was harsh, but it was the truth. If I died I would be leaving behind my almost 12-year-old daughter. If I died, our twins would die. If I died, Tim would become a widower. My family couldn't live a great life without their beloved Kween. So, I *decided* to live. I looked at Tim again, grabbed his hand and said, "let's do this."

It was at that moment that I *decided* to survive. I *decided* I had to do this surgery. I *decided* that I would do everything in my power to also save our twins.

The doctor made arrangements for me to be checked into the hospital and before I was registered and assigned a room, something happened. The pain was now at a 100 on a scale of 1-10 (yes, girl, you read that right). I could no longer walk so I had to use a wheelchair. I remember there was a small bump as the carpet transitioned to tile flooring and I thought I would pass out. The pain was so unbearable that as soon as I got in the room the doctors gave me two shots of morphine and it did absolutely NOTHING for the pain.

I was on injectable blood thinners to prevent blood clots, so the surgeon initially wanted to wait until the next morning to operate. But after a second ultrasound, the surgeon informed me they would have to perform the operation immediately. As I picked up the phone to call my employer, the surgeon told me there wasn't enough time to make that call, so Tim had to call my employer, parents and a few of my best friends; Ej, Kristie, Darlene, and Shandrea.

What was supposed to be a 30-minute procedure took almost 2 hours. Tim was frantic during this time, and the fact that this date fell on the same date his mother passed away, nine years earlier was eery for him.

A little over two hours later, I woke up and the first question I asked the nurses was, "Are my babies ok"?

She assured me they were and said Tim was waiting to see me. I continued to about the babies, so she offered me the option of using a fetal heart monitor to give me added assurance. I jumped at the opportunity. I had a vertical incision, and it was painful but I heard the sweet sounds of my babies' heartbeats and that gave me instant joy.

Later the next day, when I was in my room recovering, there were additional complications and it caused the doctors to place a tube down my nose, and into my stomach. The doctor also explains the mass was actually a cyst that was the size of a softball and it had completely cut off oxygen to my right ovary and fallopian tube. The surgeon had to remove my entire right ovary and fallopian tube. In addition, after testings, it was confirmed there was a THIRD baby in my fallopian tubes. Therefore, the twins were actually triplets and one baby didn't make it.

After learning this news, a superior at my place of employment called me to find out when I would be returning to work. I was floored! How dare this person call me and ask when I would be returning to work? This person was well aware that I had just had life-saving surgery! I was angry, so at that moment I *decided* I would only work for someone that has common decency, respect and compassion. I knew I would only get that for sure, from myself. So in that moment, I *decided* I would not return to Corporate America after the birth of my babies.

Life Lesson For Business:

No one will go hard for you, like you! And if you sit back and wait for opportunity, you may wait forever. Don't be a little bitch. Decide what you want and go after it. No excuses.

Action Step:

Take out your journal and decide right now, what you will and/or will not do. Write it down and be matter of fact with your thoughts and ideas. Put today's date and *decide* when you want to start and/or achieve this mission. Make sure you keep it updated and continue to keep track of your progress and experience. Feel free to share this goal with me by emailing me at Kween@KweenMingo.com.

Affirmation #5

I am fierce, fabulous, and fearless.

Chapter 5

Girl, Don't Be Scurred (Scared)

What has you so terrified? Be honest with yourself. What is your biggest fear when it comes to starting your business? Are you afraid your plans won't go the way you imagined? Are you afraid you aren't ready to move forward? Are you afraid to leave your job? What is the real fear that is keeping you from pursuing your dreams?

I have been a business consultant for quite some time now, and I have worked with people in many different industries. I have worked with attorneys, hair salon owners, paralegals, t-shirt vendors and so much more. The one thing that is relatively consistent with almost all of my clients is their fear of failure.

Failure is an illusion that doesn't exist.

Let's put this in a real-life example. December 31, 2017, I made a goal of helping seven people earn $100,000 or more in 2018 with their business venture. Now, I wasn't sure

HOW I would go about doing so or if anyone would even want me to help them (as we all know people can be skeptical). As of right now, June 8, 2018, I have helped three people accomplish this goal.

There are six more FULL months left in 2018, so there is a possibility I will accomplish this goal. But there is also a possibility that I won't. For the sake of this chapter, let's assume I only help five people earn $100,000 this year. Will I have failed? In short, no.

I will have successfully helped five people earn $100,000 or more and to those five people, I would have successfully accomplished my purpose. Now, you may be thinking, "but Kween, you didn't meet your goal!"

Not meeting your goal, isn't a failure. It is another opportunity to try things a different way. Sure, we all make mistakes but mistakes are not a sign of failure. It's a sign that you are pursuing something new and different. So of course there will mistakes made on the path to pursuing my goals, but there is always a lesson to be learned. Take these lessons and use them to make yourself better.

Life Lesson For Business:

If failure is an illusion, I can't fail. So, make mistakes. Make as many mistakes as I want. Make mistakes often. Bask in the joy of making mistakes. Making mistakes means I am making progress. Just don't make excuses.

Action Plan:

Let's get down to the nitty-gritty and get specific about your goals. Think about what you want to achieve. Get your notebook and as specific as possible, write down your goals as if you have already reached them, AND acknowledge your fears.

So, for example, you may want to say something like, *"After debating with myself for two long years, I've finally decided to open a health and wellness spa. It was scary because I didn't think I would be able to hire enough staff but I am so happy now that I have done so because business is thriving."*

Take a picture of this journal entry with your phone and whenever you get scared, read this to yourself!

Affirmation #6

I believe in myself. Doubt cannot live within me.

Chapter 6

Don't Doubt Yourself

Girl! Let me take you back to 1997.

When I was in the 7th grade, I played Volleyball. Now, girl! I was HORRIBLE! I doubt I would have even made the team, but there were no tryouts since they barely had enough players for the team.

Anyway, back to me being a horrible volleyball player; Whenever I would serve the ball, I could never get the thing over the stupid net. It was just terrible!! So, during the game, when it was my turn to serve the ball, my coach would pull me out of the game. It became routine so I expected him to pull me out when my turn came to serve the ball.

One day, when it was my turn to serve the ball during a game, my coach did not pull me out of the game. I looked nervously at him and his assistant, and they still didn't pull me out of the game. I wanted to cry right then and there. I looked over at my cousin, who also played - and she was GREAT at ALL sports -

and she just looked at me like, "girl, what are you going to do?" So in that moment, I remembered everything I had learned in practice - but not yet mastered - and I served the ball!

Guess what? The ball went over the net!!! That was the FIRST time that had ever happened! I felt so liberated! I felt like I was on top of the world! I felt like I finally had my shit together! I don't even remember if we scored that round. I just know the ball went over the net and it placed me on cloud 9. My entire team was proud of me. And we were all shocked.

Often we psych ourselves into believing we aren't worthy. We think just because a situation didn't work in our favor previously, it won't ever work for us. This isn't the case! Sometimes, it takes someone else to believe in you before you can see your full potential. Just look at my 12-year-old self! It took my coaches' belief in me (or at least appearing to believe in me) for me to serve the ball and get it over the net. Well, girlfriend, I am here to tell you, I BELIEVE IN YOU! And you might be thinking, "how can you believe in me when you don't even know me? Girl, bye!" Well, I believe in you. And not like the cheesy "oh, you can do it, I know you can" mumbo jumbo! I believe in you because I know if I can achieve my dreams - me, the girl who got pregnant at 15, the girl who was told she would never be anything more than someone who pops out multiple babies by random men, the girl who has always been the underdog - then YOU CAN TOO.

Life Lesson For Business:

Don't doubt yourself. Take chances on yourself. You have all the tools you need to handle anything your life and your business throws your way. Just be mindful of your thoughts. Whenever you feel the need to doubt yourself, remember you have the power to boss up and handle it. Make no excuses.

Action Plan:

Be super mindful of your thoughts. If you notice you're saying things to yourself that you wouldn't say to your best friend, say out loud, "NOPE! NOT TODAY!" then think of something else. Anything positive or anything that brings a smile to your face.

If you find yourself panicking due to a pending deadline or bills mounting up, use the same method and say out loud, "NOPE! NOT TODAY!" and then think positive thoughts and happy thoughts.

Make it your mission to say positive thoughts to yourself throughout the entire day. If you notice you are saying derogatory and negative stuff to yourself, feel free to write it in your journal. Then, make a note of what is going on at that moment when you are thinking these thoughts. Write down how it makes you feel. And then write down an alternative thought, but a positive one. Practice this daily.

Affirmation #7

My life gets more and more fabulous every day.

Chapter 7

Do You, Boo!

I graduated from East Lake High School in Tarpon Springs, Florida (GO EAGLES!) in May of 2003. Man! That was such a wonderful time because I walked that stage with a child on my hip! Not literally but figuratively. My baby girl was in the crowd, cheering me on! It was a momentous occasion because so many people did not believe in me.

I had a teacher, who isn't worthy of being mentioned by name, who would verbally attack me every single chance she got! I remember one day, we had to do a project that is very similar to a vision board. We had to cut out pictures of what we wanted our future to look like and attach them to a poster board. We then presented our boards to the class.

One thing I had on my board was my plans to go to college and become wildly successful. I don't remember my full presentation, but I do remember ending it with a world famous quote by the former head of

The United Negro College Fund, Arthur Fletcher, "A mind is a terrible thing to waste."

When everyone was finished presenting to the class, the teacher decided to critique everyone. But in my opinion, my critique was the only one that was littered with criticism. I remember she gave this long, drawn out and overwhelmingly uneducated response. She went on and on and on about knowing several millionaire business owners who had not graduated from high school and yet were *wildly successful* (did you catch that subtle piece?).

So, she goes on a little more and she says something along the lines of, "I don't know why people think 'knowledge is power' because you don't have to graduate from high school to have knowledge, so that is dumb to say."

Ok, so first of all, she tried to shade me but used the wrong quote. Second of all, what? That was just not a smart thing to say! Of course, you can be very knowledgeable with limited education BUT knowledge *is* power! Whether it's the knowledge you gain from schooling, the knowledge you gain from living in the streets, the knowledge you gain from your errors in life or the knowledge you get just from reading this book, KNOWLEDGE IS POWER!

I personally have gotten first-hand accounts (knowledge) of the direct impacts of slavery, Jim Crow, and so much directly from my great-grandmother, whose grandmother was a slave. She was able to give me the real deal information that you aren't taught in school. So, I agree all knowledge doesn't have to come from schooling but knowledge is still power.

Life Lesson For Business:

Everyone won't see your vision. Everyone won't agree with you. Everyone won't want to work with you. Don't let that stop you. Continue to pursue your passions until you make history. Know your worth. Make no excuses.

Action Plan:

Vision Board

Pull out those old magazines and books (you can also print images from the internet). Find pictures/images that describes the contributions you would like to make to the world. Find pictures of things that represent what goes on in your head and/or heart and depicts the life you want to live. What materialistic things would you like? And don't get shy and limit yourself based upon what other people's opinions. If you want to drop $250,000 on a vehicle, don't worry about your mom, sister, cousin, uncle or anyone else saying, "I would never spend that kind of money on a car". DO YOU, BOO!

Once you have those pictures together, get a poster board, cardboard or any other board you have handy and place your images on the board. Put your board somewhere you will see it every day. As you achieve your goals, add more to your vision board.

Affirmation #8

*I will win, and I will clap for my damn self
during the entire process.*

Chapter 8

Keep That Shit To Yourself, Sis

When you're excited about something, it's easy to want to share your excitement with people closest to you. But there isn't much that can make you second guess and doubt your dreams and ambitions quicker than a Negative Nancy. We've all been there and so I have learned to keep shit to myself.

Currently, no one knows I am even writing this book. Not my husband, not my children, not my best friends, not my parents or anyone else. Just me and God. I chose not to tell anyone because I don't need any negative energy. I don't need anyone putting their limited thoughts and beliefs onto me. Of course, *most* people mean well but that isn't necessarily what's best for you or me.

Let me ask you a question: have you ever had such exciting news to tell a close friend, like losing weight, hitting your financial goal, getting promoted, etc. and their response made you wish you had never told them? How did that make you feel?

Now, that very feeling is why you should keep shit to yourself, sis!

When I decided to seek medical help after not being able to conceive, I couldn't wait to tell a few friends. One person stands out because of this person's poor attitude. For the sake of privacy, let's call this person Bones.

Bones and I were super close, so naturally, I wanted to tell Bones how excited I was to see a specialist. And since Bones and I were so close, she was well aware of my issues, outside of my infertility problems. I thought this would make this moment even more exciting.

The day Bones and I had lunch after work, I was so thrilled and beaming with happiness because I felt Tim and I were going to be one step closer to having another baby. When Bones' drink arrived at our table, I broke the news. I excitedly explained I found a specialist who would run tests and help me find out why we hadn't conceived yet. As I went on about the possibilities of seeing a doctor, Bones looked unamused.

After spilling the beans, I told Bones I was at wits ends and adoption will be our next choice in the event things don't work out and the doctor isn't able to give me answers. Without missing a beat, Bones looked me square in the eyes and said, "you might as well move on to adoption because it is clear, you won't be giving birth again."

I was crushed. In that split second, my entire body felt numb. All my hopes and dreams were vanishing at that moment because Bones had a bad attitude with no faith.

On the way home, I kept thinking, "Bones is probably right. I got pregnant with Kianna so easily, so I probably won't ever have another baby."

I began to doubt everything, all because I didn't keep that shit to myself and wanted a Negative Nancy to share in my happiness. But as you know, I pushed that negativity to the back of my brain and kept going. Her words still lingered like the smell of a dirty diaper sitting in the back of a hot car, but I was able to move forward and not tell her anything else. And when I did get pregnant again, she found out through Facebook. There was no need in me telling her the great news because she probably would have said something about me having miscarriages. Who needs that negativity in their life? I sure as hell don't!

Don't allow the *Bones* in your life to make you doubt yourself. Keep that shit to yourself sis and clap for your damn self!

Life Lessons For Business:

Nobody needs to know the route you take to make things happen. Just shut up, show up and show out. Let your results do the talking. No excuses.

Action Plan:

A personal motto/mission statement can keep you focused when you get discouraged (because we all get discouraged, honey!). Let's come up with a personal motto/mission statement just for you! So, pull out your journal and let's get started.

Take out a stopwatch or your phone. Set the timer for 90 seconds. During this time, make a list of words that describe you. It can be any word as long as it represents you. Once you are finished, look at your list. Is there a common theme? How are the words related? Once you have this info, on another page in your journal, begin to freewrite. I want you to write anything about yourself for 10 minutes using the words on your list.

Now, using your list of words and your 10 minutes of freewriting, what words and statement stand out to you the most? Using that info, draft your personal motto/mission statement. Don't worry, you can change it at any time but always keep it close to you for reference in the future.

Affirmation #9

I love myself, and I won't ever steer myself wrong.

Chapter 9

F*** Their Feelings

My intuition hasn't failed me yet. In the past, whenever I sensed something, I was usually right. I honestly, can't think of one time that my intuition was wrong but even so, I have gone against my intuition and it left me in a bad position.

After graduating high school in 2003, I decided I would pursue my dream of attending Florida Agricultural and Mechanical University (FAMU). I delayed one semester because I needed to get everything in order for my daughter. So, I opted to enroll spring semester instead of fall.

Even after waiting a semester, I still knew I wouldn't be able to take my daughter to school with me immediately. Fortunately, my parents were agreeable to caring for Kianna while I got things in order during my first semester of college.

From the moment my parents dropped me off at my apartment on campus and drove off, I knew this wasn't the best decision for my daughter. I began to feel selfish. There were plenty of colleges in The Tampa Bay area, and I got accepted into every college I applied for, including the colleges in The Tampa Bay area. So, why did I opt to leave my daughter four hours away? My gut feeling was telling me this was all wrong, but I let my ego get the best of me because didn't want to prove other people right by quitting college.

Nine days after I arrived on campus, Kianna got really sick. I took the last few dollars I had in my bank account, and I purchased a one-way bus ticket to Clearwater, Florida. That was one of the longest rides of my life. I hated it, but I was so happy when I saw my daughter's beautiful smile when I got home.

Kianna was suffering from a severe upper respiratory infection and required antibiotics. Once she was well, about two weeks later, my mom, her best friend and Kianna drove me back to Tallahassee. That entire four hour-drive felt like doom was lingering in the air. Every time I looked at my daughter, I wanted to burst into tears. It was horrible.

When we pulled up at my apartment, I wanted to kick and scream like a two-year-old having a tantrum. The feeling I had in the pit of my stomach made me want to vomit. As the day went on, I knew it was a matter of time before my mom and her best friend left with Kianna in tow. When the moment finally arrived, I tried to remain strong. It wasn't until everyone was in the car, seat belted and ready to go that I almost lost my shit. Like full on, lost my shit. But, I held it together. That is until my daughter looked at me with her eyes saying, "Mommy, are you coming?" as she reached her little hands to me that I finally did it. I became that two-year-old, having a complete meltdown. I cried and begged my mom not to leave me. And after about 2.7 seconds of debating, we both agreed that I should go home with them, despite the fact we knew my dad would be pissed.

I don't regret making that decision. Returning home to my daughter was the best thing I could have done, other than never leaving her behind in the first place. I no longer cared that my dad would be upset. I didn't care if people mocked me for "dropping out of college". I didn't care what anyone thought. I just had to be with my daughter.

You may be asking yourself, "What the hell does this have to do with starting my business?" Well, it has a lot to do with it. This single day in my life taught me a valuable business lesson; do what you have to do, regardless of who it pisses off. Of course, you want to keep your morals in tact but if you're not harming anyone, don't worry about their feelings. Do what you need to do.

Life Lesson For Business:

If you're not bringing harm to anyone else, f*** their feelings. Make no excuses.

Action Plan:

Take out that notebook and look at your passions from Chapter 2. Using this information, write down five long-term goals and three short-term goals based upon your intuition. Then for each goal write out 3-5 action steps to get started on these goals. For example, if your goal is to make $5,000 more per month. Three action steps could be:

1. Sell my expertise
2. Raise prices of my product line
3. Add new products to clothing line

This is just an example so tailor it to fit your needs. Just make sure it is what YOU want to do.

Affirmation #10

Beyoncé is my spirit animal. I will win at everything.

Chapter 10

What Would Beyoncé Do?

It's no big secret that I am a full on Beyoncé fan! Beyond that, it is one of my lifelong dreams to not only meet her but have a conversation with her *fingers crossed and speaking it into existence*.

I almost came close to meeting her during the 2016 White House Easter Egg Roll, but I literally missed her by like 2 minutes! Girl, I am still regretting that.

So, daily we are all faced with different tasks that can help better our lives but what do we do? We all tend to put things off.

So to combat this, I have a post-it note on my computer that says, "What would Beyoncé do?"

I feel in my bones that Beyoncé is the epitome of the hardest working HUMAN alive (and I have to say LeBron James is a close second). I mean good grief, Beyoncé gave birth to twins and then in a year or so, she is onstage giving us all LIFE and snatching all our edges! Homegirl IS THE BUSINESS! OK?!

Beyoncé doesn't wait for the "right time". Beyoncé doesn't wait until Friday. Beyoncé doesn't wait until summer. Beyoncé doesn't wait until things feels right. No, Beyoncé makes a plan and handles her shit. Beyoncé practices her art until it is as perfect as any human can get. Beyoncé handles her responsibilities. Beyoncé does what needs to be done without making excuses. Beyoncé puts in *werk*! This is why Beyoncé is Beyoncé and why I love her and so many others look up to her.

Life Lesson For Business:

When shit goes down and life throws you lemons, make an album and shut the haters up. No excuses.

Action Plan:

In chapter 2, I asked you about your role model. Now, I want you to go a bit deeper. I want you to make a list of all the qualities you love about this person.

Are there any qualities that you would like to adopt? What qualities does your role model have, that you can use to help improve and/or get started with your business?

For example:

Beyoncé
1. Gets shit done
2. Go-getter
3. Passionate mother
4. Relatively private life
5. She rarely (if ever) responds to negativity
6. She loves her body
7. She will LITERALLY fall and get right back up as if nothing happened! She doesn't miss a beat!
8. She is charitable
9. She is relentless in pursuit of her goals
10. Even though she is a MEGASTAR, she surprisingly seems relatable

I just listed ten but there are a billion more great qualities Beyoncé possess. And of these ten, the ones I need to work on for my businesses are:

1. Have a more private life.
   a. Maybe I should chill with posting on Instagram but I always feel like it is small things I post that can give someone else hope, love and encouragement. So, I should stick to the ultimate goal and not post a lot of personal pictures.
2. Don't respond to negativity (with some exceptions because I do believe in addressing customer/client complaints).
3. Love my body.
   a. After having Kam, I have struggled with my body image. I have an image in my head of how my body should look and I want to achieve this goal. However, sometimes, I do need to understand I gave

birth to four humans and I have breastfed my four babies. Things are headed south, and that is just a natural part of life.

4. She falls and gets her ass right back up

    a. We all fall - NOT to be confused with fail, which is an illusion. But Beyoncé will physically fall and get back up as if nothing happened. She doesn't miss a beat. This is super important in business because when we do "fall," it is essential to get back up and keep on going like nothing ever happened.

5. Beyoncé is relatable.

    a. Remember in business, people buy from those they know, like and trust. Start by being relatable.

Affirmation #11

Gratitude is my attitude!

Chapter 11

Embrace The Unexpected

March of 2016, I had an annual "lady parts" exam. My doctor did the usual full work up, and he said because of my issues with PCOS, severe scar tissues and endometriosis, I wouldn't be able to conceive again. For me, it wasn't that big of a deal because I felt incredibly blessed with my three children. I was grateful for my babies, so I wasn't upset and just carried on with my business as usual. I honestly don't remember telling Tim what the doctor said. He says I told him, but it wasn't a big deal to me, so I didn't think much of it.

About a week later, Kianna and I went on a few tour dates with Tim and his artist. We ended up going to The White House Easter Egg Roll on one of the dates (this is where I missed the opportunity to meet Beyoncé by a few moments - UGH!). We had a fantastic time. First Lady Michelle Obama waved at me and I even got that on camera! It was so exciting, and a wonderful occasion.

While in Washington, DC, I was able to show my daughter all these beautiful statues and monuments. She enjoyed it, and so did I. It was simply a great time.

When we got back home to Atlanta, life went on. I was signing attorneys for my paralegal company. I was continuing to rank well with my network marketing company. My 501(c)3 nonprofit organization, Konfidence of a Kween, was doing well. And most importantly, my children were doing well. We were traveling a lot and just living life to the fullest.

I had recently started working out at the gym to lose a few pounds after having the twins so when my menstrual cycle was late, I attributed it to my body adjusting to me working out.

One day at the gym, my trainer had me doing planks. For some reason, I wanted to hurl my entire breakfast. It didn't feel like morning sickness or anything. I just felt like perhaps I didn't thoroughly cook my breakfast. But then I started to think to myself, "what if I am pregnant?" Then I laughed at myself.

On the way home, I just kept thinking, "go get a pregnancy test", so I did. But girl! I was not about to spend $15 on a pregnancy test just for it to be negative. I just really wanted to take it so I didn't continue to have this nagging feeling. So, I did what any sensible person would do; I stopped by Dollar Tree and got a pregnancy test.

When I got home, I didn't even tell Tim about the pregnancy test. I just kissed him, and went straight upstairs to shower and take this stupid test.

After I handled my business, I sat on the toilet. Naked. Waiting for the urine to run across the little window. Well, the side where the test shows positive popped up before the control line. So, my immediate thought was, "stupid ass pregnancy test! The control line is on the wrong side!"

I thought the test malfunctioned or something, but then 5 seconds later, something miraculous happened. The second line popped up. I sat there stunned for a moment, wondering if the test was right. And then it hit me; I'M PREGNANT.

I was so shocked and excited that I ran out of the bathroom, butt booty naked, knocking over the paper cup of urine. I got to the catwalk and looked down into our living room and yelled to Tim, "BABE! BABE! WE DID IT! WE ARE PREGNANT!!"

Tim jumped up and said, "for real?"

I replied, "hell yeah!"

We were both in shock but happy! After having so many issues with getting pregnant, suffering miscarriages and then finally giving birth to our twins, only to be told we can no longer have more children, this was music to our ears. And since I had discovered baby aspirin can help me carry my babies to term, I immediately popped a baby aspirin and then called my doctor.

When I went in to confirm the pregnancy, my doctor walked in and said, "CONGRATULATIONS!" He proceeded to tell me how far along we were and the baby's due date, etc.

I did the math in my head and then I chuckled to myself. I told him, going by these dates, I got pregnant exactly eight days after he told me I couldn't have any more children. He smiled and said, "It's science, girl. I'm not God!"

And just like that, God showed me after praying and putting in the work, you have to be patient.

I went through years of trying to conceive, only to end up have multiple miscarriages. And while I could never replace the four babies I lost (remember, my first set of twins, my son and the baby that was stuck in my fallopian tubes), I am grateful for the four babies that I was blessed to birth.

Nothing is set in stone when it comes to this crazy world. Things will change. Things will happen unexpectedly. But it's how you handle the unexpected that will shape your life. Embrace the unexpected and don't miss a beat.

Life Lesson For Business:

Things will come up. Plans will change. People will cancel on you. Just make up for your losses, continue to prepare for the unexpected and roll with the punches. Don't give up. Make no excuses.

Action Plan:

Pull out your journal. Once a day, every day for 30 days, write down at least one thing you're grateful for in life. When you're feeling discouraged, review your list.

Affirmation #12

*I lay down the burden of doubt, shame, guilt, and
embarrassment. I will love myself and
forgive myself.*

Chapter 12

Quantrell

I remember the day I first met my little brother, Quantrell. I didn't like him. My four-year-old little brain couldn't understand why I had to share the spotlight with this loud baby. I don't think I was prepared for what would happen when he entered this world. I don't believe anyone explained to me what would happen when the baby was no longer "in mommy's belly."

I remember having this image in my head that I would meet my new baby brother, and he would come crawling to me. I would pick him up and play with him and then he would go back into mommy's belly. But, he was here to stay whether I liked it or not.

Once Quantrell could talk, I began to like him. He would follow me around and ask questions. There were many days, I would have to come up with random answers to crazy questions like, "why does grass smell so bad?"

I remember teaching Quantrell how to ride his bike. Everything was all good until he hit a pothole and fell off, busting his lip open (I still feel bad about that and it was almost 25 years ago).

I remember reading to him every night before bedtime because I loved reading and wanted to share my love for reading with him.

When I got pregnant with Kianna, he was only 11-years-old, but he was so excited. He tried to convince my dad to buy a bunch of baby stuff the day he found out I was pregnant. And when I gave birth, he was there the entire time until I was wheeled back to the operating room.

When Kianna was older, Quantrell began treating her like she was his little sister, and they became super close. They started to act alike and look alike. It was so weird but also refreshing.

When I moved to Atlanta, I would go back home to visit often. During these times, I would hang out and party with my friends. Quantrell and I would try to beat each other back home to our parents' house because the first one there was able to sleep in Quantrell's bed. The person who came in later had to sleep on the couch. I usually would win, and even if I didn't, I would make him get out of the bed so I could sleep.

Every single time we would see each other, I would not allow him to leave me until he gave a big hug, kiss on the cheek and we said, "I love you."

We simply had a strong and loving bond.

November 24, 2013, Quantrell sent me a Facebook message with his new phone number. Here is exactly how the conversation went:

- 4:06 pm
    - Sis u got My new #
- 4:06pm
    - Send it to me I'm on phone w mama talking bout u now
- 4:07pm
    - 8134109***

I didn't call him.

November 27, 2013, at about 6:20 am, I was lying in bed thinking I should call my job and not go to work when my phone began to ring. Usually, my phone ringer is off but for some reason, it wasn't off on this particular morning.

I rolled over and saw it was my mom calling. So I said to Tim, "it's just my mom."

I debated about answering the phone because my mom can be a bit dramatic and I didn't want to listen to her complain at that hour, but at the last minute I picked up the phone.

"Hey ma," I said slightly annoyed.

She was crying and said, "Kia! They shot him! They shot him!"

"Who? What are you talking about", I said, now concerned.

"Quantrell! They shot him," she said crying profusely.

I am usually the levelheaded person when shit goes down, so I always try to remain calm even in the most tumultuous situations. So it was no surprise when I replied, "ok ma, where is he?" because in my head, he had to be at the hospital getting treatment. I even already had it in my head that I would punch him for scaring everybody like this. But I wasn't prepared for my mom's response.

"No! They killed him! They killed my baby", she screamed.

All I could do was shake Tim and tell him what happened as I cried.

I didn't want to tell Kianna what had happened because I knew it would crush
her. I also knew she would have questions that I couldn't answer. But after speaking with Tim, we told her what happened and we watched our baby girl's heart break into a million pieces.

It took the police longer than expected to release my brother's body, so it took well over a week for the funeral services. That was the most exhausting and emotional week of my life. Just knowing you have to do this daunting task but you are forced to prolong the process was enough to give me daily migraines.

December 4, 2013, our family buried Quantrell. I recited a poem. Our older sister, Tonya spoke a few words about our brother. We had cousins who also spoke a few words. And everyone was heartbroken. Everyone.

One of my biggest regrets is not calling him when he sent me his new phone number. I just thought to myself, "eh! We will talk on Thanksgiving". But he didn't live to get that call.

At the time of me writing this book, it's been almost five years and police still haven't arrested anyone in connection with my brother's murder. The only information we have is what was provided on The Pasco County Sheriff's Office Facebook Page, that reads:

Cold Case:

Cold Case Homicide, Victim- Quantrell Keller

Remembrance for Murder

On November 26, 2013, Quantrell Keller was staying at [****] Rosedale Lane in Holiday, Florida. Around 11:00 P.M., Keller was shot in the doorway of the home and the suspect fled the scene. Keller was taken to the hospital, but later passed away from his injuries.

The suspect is described as a stocky, Hispanic male who may be between the ages of 20 and 30 years old. That night the suspect was wearing a dark hooded sweatshirt. A witness described the suspect as having a round face.

Keller was known to frequent [nightclubs] in both Pasco and Pinellas counties.

If you have any information please contact Sgt. Hatcher at jhatcher@pascosheriff.org or Det. Meizo at cmeizo@pascosheriff.org. To be eligible for up to a $3,000 reward, please contact the Tampa Bay Crimestoppers at 1-800-873-TIPS or submit a tip online: https://www.p3tips.com/TipForm.aspx?ID=155&P3ID=155&DSID=155.

To honor my brother, Tim and I named two of our children after him. It is also my understanding a close friend of his, also named her son after my brother.

Everyone loved Quantrell. Everyone misses him. My sister and I often speak of him and reminisce about the fond memories we had.

I've come to accept the fact this case may remain a cold case forever. But I also realize someone who knows something about Quantrell's murder will read this book. I hope and pray you do the right thing and tell someone. You can even email me at Kween@KweenMingo.com. We just want justice for Quantrell.

There are days I get angry all over again. I get annoyed when I think about the fact that no one has been held accountable for their actions. I get upset that my brother can't celebrate my accomplishments. I get sad because I won't ever be able to celebrate any more of his accomplishments. My heart aches for my children, three of whom will never get to meet their uncle. My family was robbed of the love of my brother. My brother was robbed of his life and the opportunity to live life to its full potential. The world was robbed of a man who had the potential to change the entire universe.

Life Lesson Learned For Business:

Act Now! Don't wait. Don't procrastinate. No matter how big or how small the task is, do it and get it out of the way. Don't end up regretting your missed opportunity.

Make every moment of every day count. Once those precious seconds have passed, you will never get them back.

Love your family and friends. Support your family and friends. Apologize when you are wrong. Forgive when they are wrong. Don't keep count of wrongdoings. If you're upset, get over it and move on.

Gently release anger and rage from your body. Nothing good will come from these feelings. Instead, choose to use compassion, love, and understanding.

Release any shame you are harboring.

Find your inner peace by forgiving yourself and loving yourself.

Live life to the absolute fullest.

Make no excuses.

Action Plan:

Make a to-do list of all the things you need to get done. Do this for your daily tasks, weekly tasks, monthly tasks and so on. Cross each item off your list as you get them done. At the end of the day/week/month, bask in your accomplishments.

Bonus Action Plan:

Make a list of all the things you do every single day of your life. Then, make a list of all the things you love to do. Compare your two lists. Adjust your lists accordingly.

Life is too short to do things you hate.

Acknowledgments

First and foremost, I have to thank God. I've never had the desire to fit into the crowd, and I have always embraced the quirks I've been blessed to have.

I also must acknowledge my husband, Tim aka Booface. Thank you for always encouraging me and pushing me to be my best. Thank you for being an excellent provider and protector. Life has been a rollercoaster for us, but it has been a thrill that I wouldn't want to experience with anyone else but you. I love you.

My oldest child, Kianna. I love you so much. You are the most patient and humble child I know. I see the passion in your eyes when you play basketball, and I want you to know I believe in you and your dream. I will always support you! Thank you for always understanding when mommy had to work late or go to class early. Thank you for making me feel like the best mom ever, even when I wasn't so deserving. Thank you for being my DoDa Bug.

Timia, my princess. When I look at you, I see myself. You're such a girlie girl and quirky, like me. I see your drive and ambition even at such a young age. I see the passion in your eyes when you put your mind to something. Keep going. Don't ever quit. Mommy will always love you.

Timothy, Jr, my knight in shining armor. If you would have had the chance to meet your Uncle Quantrell, you would probably be visiting him every chance you got. Your sense of humor is a carbon copy of your uncle's sense of humor. It's ok to be a clown but remember there is always a time and a place. Mommy loves you forever and ever.

Kam The Man! From the moment, you were conceived, you have been full of surprises. Your energy is like no other. Even as a one-year-old baby, your personality still stands out and shines through. The way you remain steadfast in your convictions is enviable (even if it is your tantrums when you want your juice). I love you dearly, and I am looking forward to helping you pursue your passions.

To my parents, thank you so much for teaching me about this crazy world. I would not have survived without your help. You helped me raise Kianna like she was your own child. And then, when I had the twins, you guys backed up and moved to Atlanta to help me. I love you so much and I appreciate you.

To all my big head siblings, thank you for the laughs and the cries. I couldn't have asked for a better sister than Tonya. You taught me how to be tough, so the world wouldn't see me sweat. I love you so much. To my brothers, thank you all for always having my back. Thank you for being tough on me but loving to me as well. I love you all, and I am so proud to call yall my siblings.

To my grandparents, aunts, uncles, and cousins, thanks for being the village that raised this kid. I love yall!

To my friends, thanks for the support and for pushing me when needed. Thanks for encouraging me to handle my shit and not make any excuses. Thank you for forcing me to take vacations so I don't get overwhelmed. Yall the real MVPs. I love yall.

And to you, reading this book; THANK YOU for taking a chance and using your valuable time to read my book. I am so thankful and appreciative that I can't entirely put gratitude into words. I pray you have found this book to be valuable and you surpass your wildest dreams. Whenever you feel discouraged, go back and look at all your journal entries and remember I LOVE YOU. I APPRECIATE YOU. I VALUE YOU. I BELIEVE IN YOU!

LOOK MA! WE MADE IT!

Works Cited

Dora The Explorer. Nickelodeon Studios, 14 August 2000.

About the Author

Kween Mingo is the founder and registered trademark owner of The Kweendom™, an online platform dedicated to helping other women discover their passions and turn it into a paycheck.

Working as a paralegal for well over a decade, Kween has helped attorneys amass an estimated $50 million in attorney fees. After having an epiphany, Kween decided to help other women discover their passions and earn a lucrative income. She gets joy out of helping other people solve business problems.

When Kween isn't helping other people start and/or build their businesses, you can find her flipping houses or vacationing with her family.

Contact/Join The Kweendom™:

Join Our Facebook group -
https://www.facebook.com/groups/173405476379594/

Follow me on Instagram -
https://www.instagram.com/kweenofduhworld/

Email me: Kween@KweenMingo.com

Work with me, book me for speaking engagements, get notification of new book releases. -
https://freedomofthekweendom.com/more-info/

Thank you for reading book one of the No Bullshitting Series!

Kween Mingo

The Kweendom™

Made in the USA
Lexington, KY
23 June 2018